D0124647

Keeping
a Journal

Trudi Strain Trueit

Franklin Watts
A Division of Scholastic Inc.
New York • Toronto • London • Auckland • Sydney
Mexico City • New Delhi • Hong Kong
Danbury, Connecticut

Dedication
For my brother, Dean—friend, dreamer, and
faithful keeper of childhood pacts

Cover design by John Gibson.
Interior design by Kathleen Santini.
Photos by the 1,000 Journals Project.

Excerpt p. 40 reprinted from *The Diary of a Young Girl, the Definitive Edition* by Anne Frank. Otto H. Frank & Mirjam Pressler, Editors, translated by Susan Massotty, copyright © 1995 by Doubleday, a division of Random House, Inc. Used by permission of Doubleday, a division of Random House, Inc.

Library of Congress Cataloging-in-Publication Data

Trueit, Trudi Strain.
   Keeping a journal / Trudi Strain Trueit.
      v. cm. — (Life balance)
Includes bibliographical references and index.
Contents: Navigating the journey—Why journal?—Time travel—Getting started—Write now!—A 30-Day journal.
      ISBN 0-531-12262-X (lib. bdg.)   0-531-15581-1 (pbk.)
      1. Diaries—Authorship. [1. Diaries—Authorship. 2. English language—Composition and exercises.] I. Title. II. Series.
   PN4390.T78 2003
   808'.06692—dc22
                              2003025290

Table of Contents

Navigating the Journey

My first journal was a pocket-size, hot pink book with "diary" written across the cover in cursive, gold letters. It came with a key no bigger than a peanut to open a tiny lock so wobbly you could easily pop it with a bent paper clip, which is what I did after I lost the miniature key. At first, I hesitated to write in the journal. Every great book I'd ever read had adventure, mystery, and suspense. My life was stale tuna sandwiches, clarinet practice, and soccer games—not exactly gripping drama.

Still, a part of me was eager to see what thoughts might spill out of my head, so I took a chance. From the moment my pen moved across a sheet of paper barely thicker than a dragonfly's wing, I was free. I could say anything. Feel anything. Dream anything. In my journal, I didn't have to be a heroic character in a novel. I didn't have to be beautiful or perfect or popular. Being me was, at last, enough.

A journal is a record of feelings, thoughts, experiences, challenges, and goals from your personal point of view. It is your likes and dislikes, successes and struggles, values and viewpoints. It is what you think about, go through, cope with, and long for on your travels. Your journal is a mosaic of everything and anything that is important to you. Just like a real mosaic, where you cannot usually see the design in the artwork until you step away from the tiny bits of embedded glass, stone, and tile, so it is with a journal. Each day, you place another small piece of yourself into it. When you move back, you are able to view the full picture of your life's journey.

The word *journal* comes from the French word *jour,* meaning "the day." Similarly, the English term *diary* is taken from the Latin word for "daily": *diurnal.* Originally, a journey referred to how far a person could travel in a single day. Therefore, a journal reflected someone's written account of his or her day. A journal and a diary are the same thing, though "journal" is currently the more popular term.

Today, a journal is no longer a list of someone's daily activities. Modern journals are limited only by the imagination of their authors. The type of journal you choose, its design, and its content are all up to you. Your journal may be a spiral notebook filled with original poetry and stories, a leather-bound sketchbook of artwork, photographs tucked into a scrapbook, or an on-line journal. You may use words, drawings, photos, mementos, video, or audio to record your journey. While every journal is as unique as its owner, they all have one thing in common: Each is a true expression of the heart.

A Questioning Spirit

At age eight, a boy named Elwyn Brooks began keeping a journal. For the next twenty years, he would detail his thoughts, feelings, and struggles to overcome shyness. Elwyn Brooks grew up to be E. B. White, author of Stuart Little *and* Charlotte's Web. *In 1970, White wrote a book called* The Trumpet of the Swan. *In it, the main character, Sam Beaver, writes in his journal every night before bedtime, always ending each entry with a question so he'll have something to think about as he's drifting off to sleep. Did writer E. B. White end his own journal entries the same way? Perhaps, but we'll never know for sure. Upon his request, White's personal journals were destroyed after his death in 1985.*

A journal is for your eyes alone, unless you want to share it, so none of the usual writing rules apply; there are no instructions to follow, no topics you have to cover, no homework to turn in for a grade. You do not need to be a good speller, writer, poet, speaker, artist, or photographer. The only thing you need is a willingness to allow

A journal is for your eyes alone, so none of the usual writing rules apply; there are no instructions to follow, no topics you have to cover, no homework to turn in for a grade.

whatever happens to simply happen. Do not let your own expectations or criticisms, or those of anyone else, cloud your vision. There are only a few things you'll want to remember when journaling:

- **Be yourself.** Journaling what you think you are supposed to say instead of how you honestly feel is not being true to yourself. It defeats one of the main purposes of journaling: to unlock the real you. It may also cause you to lose interest in your journal because you aren't gaining anything real or valuable from the experience.
- **Date every entry.** A journal is a great way to remember what you thought and did from day to day and from year to year. Keeping a chronological record of your life allows you to go back and review your personal history.

- **Keep your hands off all journal entries.** Everything you journal is an important piece of who you are. Once you've made an entry, consider it written in stone. Do not edit your original entry or rip out pages to throw away. Even if you later regret what you've written, "leave it alone," advises psychologist Dr. Ellen Baker, a journal-writing consultant and author. "You don't have to go back and read it, but respect that it voiced what you felt at a particular moment in time, and let it be."

Don't worry if you aren't sure how to get started. *Keeping a Journal* will take you step-by step through the process, giving you plenty of ideas on how to create and fill your one-of-a-kind journal. As you read, keep a pen and paper handy for the writing exercises, designed to encourage you to find your individual voice while learning more about your true self. Many exercises will rescue you from writer's block, that sinking feeling that comes from staring at a blank page and not knowing what to write. Hold on to the writing exercises that you do so you can include them in your journal. The last chapter will guide you through a full month of journaling using writing prompts and ideas to jumpstart your brain. So relax and have fun charting a course as you set sail across a sea of self-discovery. Bon voyage!

Two

Why Journal?

At this moment, nearly one thousand journals are circling the globe. They are being handed from one person to the next, mailed halfway around the world, or simply left in an airport for an unsuspecting person to find. It's all part of the 1,000 Journals Project, launched by Brian Singer in the summer of 2000. The San Francisco, California, graphic designer came up with the idea while photographing graffiti on bathroom walls for a potential book. "It made sense that if there was a book, people should be encouraged to write in it, on top of the photos. Then I thought, 'Why bother with the photos at all? And what if the books traveled around? And why not one thousand of them?'"

People from Australia to Africa are filling the 6-inch by 9-inch journals with artwork, photos, advice, and stories. Anyone who gets a book can "write, draw, paste, rip, cut, glue, sew, fold, whatever—it's all good," says Singer. One journaler wrote an apology in his book and then sent it to the friend he hoped would forgive him. So far, the journals

One of 1,000 journals traveling the globe, book #920 (above) found its way into the hands of artistic journalers from New Jersey to Sweden. Journal #861 (opposite page) dropped out of sight in mid-2003 and recently resurfaced in South Carolina.

have found their way to more than thirty-five countries and to every state in the United States. Only one has been completed: Number 526 traveled from Brazil to Ireland and crisscrossed thirteen U.S. states before being returned to California. Singer doesn't know when, or even if, all the journals will find their way home. It could take five years or twenty-five years. "If fifty come back, it'll be amazing," he says. At *www.1000journals.com,* you can track the progress of the journals, peek at the entries, and sign up to possibly get one—sometimes a journaler will send a book to a person on the on-line waiting list. Someday, Singer hopes to compile the

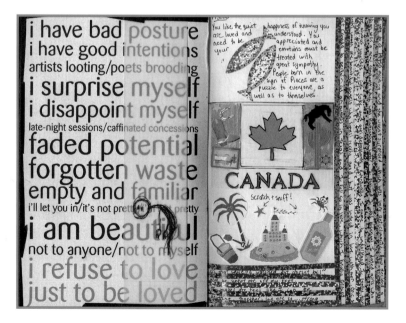

journals in a book about the project. By the time it's all over, he figures about twenty thousand lucky people around the world will have left their creative mark in the journals.

Shared journaling, like the 1,000 Journals Project, takes courage because thousands of people will see the entries. Yet personal journaling, while private, requires bravery as well. You may be afraid to start a journal because you don't think you're a good writer or maybe you don't feel there's anything in your life exciting enough to write about. Creative-writing teacher, journal keeper, and author Deborah Bouziden has heard these and dozens of other reasons for not journaling. "I tell my students this is *their* journal," she emphasizes. "They are not in competition with anyone else. It doesn't matter that they feel they can't spell or have horrific grammar. They're not writing a *New York Times* bestseller; they are recording events and thoughts about their lives. They are free to misspell and write about silly things, if that is what they feel like writing."

It isn't uncommon for young people to mistakenly believe a journal is boring. Yet, a journal can be far more than what you ate for lunch or did in science class today. Let your imagination soar. What do you secretly wish for? What have you always wanted to try? What do you dream about at night? Ask yourself questions that explore your inner thoughts, feelings, and beliefs, and you will discover you have plenty to write about—none of it boring. "Keeping a journal is an incredible way to come to know who you are; what your strengths and challenges are, what issues are hard for you, what you want to say to the world or at least to yourself, where you want to go in life, and where you've been," explains Dr. Caryn Mirriam-Goldberg, writing teacher and author. "It's one of the best gifts you can give yourself because it's totally on your own terms."

A journal can be far more than what you ate for lunch or did in science class today. What do you secretly wish for? What have you always wanted to try?

In a journal, you decide what you want to say and how you want to say it. Ask yourself if there is something that is keeping you from journaling. Maybe you simply have never before considered the benefits. As you'll soon discover, the reasons to keep a journal far outweigh the excuses not to.

Yours Truly

A journal starts out as a book of blank pages, but the moment you scribble your first word, glue in a photo, or draw a line in black ink, it becomes a part of you. In a journal, you can reveal your deepest secrets and darkest emotions, your greatest disappointments and wildest dreams. You can vent your frustrations after an argument, complain about going to your aunt's house for tofu-asparagus-rhubarb loaf, or wonder why that certain boy or girl has yet to notice you. A journal doesn't interrupt, judge, blame, or ridicule. You can be selfish, annoyed, bored, moody, illogical, fearful, furious, or indifferent—all of the things you can't always be when people are watching.

"There are always things to say that cannot be said out loud," says Charlotte, age thirteen, who started journaling a few years ago when she felt there was no one in her life she could talk to. "A lot of things are repressed when you are around people, especially people who'd rather hear you say what they want you to, rather than what is true," she explains. "I was dealing with depression, the death of a relative, and parental negligence. I had zero friends to turn to. I thought I would go crazy if I didn't let out some of my pent-up feelings and thoughts." Along with having a friend you can turn to twenty-four hours a day, seven days a week, a journal offers many other rewards.

Freedom of Expression

Much of the joy in journaling comes from being able to share yourself in any way you desire. Fill your journal with things that inspire you, from postcards and ticket stubs to pictures you've snipped out of magazines. Use colored pens and pencils, paint, glitter, stickers, stamps, and stencils to liven up your journal. Be bold. Be crazy. Be whatever you want.

For several months, peach farmer and nonfiction writer David Mas Masumoto kept a journal on why journaling was so important to him. In one entry, he wrote:

> "My journals often do not make sense. I have a rule: there can be no wrongs in my journals. I misspell words frequently, use wrong verb tenses, create sentence fragments… What's important is to get it out on paper, to commit feelings to words, to write and capture the creative spirit. I seek a freedom of expression, for no one will read these journals verbatim, my words are not intended for writing teachers or editors. No one will ever write in red ink "Who cares?" over my words. I care and that's all that matters."

To help unleash your "creative spirit," try what is called free writing. When you free-write, you let whatever thoughts, ideas, and feelings that enter your mind simply flow onto the page. You are not allowed to cross out or change anything. Free writing is also referred to as free-association writing or stream-of-consciousness writing. In free writing, there is no time to critique your work, be concerned with writing rules, or erase something you think might be wrong. You are able to express yourself without any limits.

Free Your Mind

To free-write, get a piece of notebook paper and a pen. Set a timer or alarm clock for three minutes. Start the clock. Begin writing whatever thoughts pop into your head: the weather, your pet, a hobby, your foot, a cool word—anything. Don't worry about spelling, grammar, or punctuation. Don't cross out anything. And whatever you do, don't stop. Make a list of words if you want to, but keep going. If your mind goes blank, simply scrawl your name until something else strikes you (and it will).

When the timer goes off, stop and read what you've written. Some of it may make sense. Some of it may not. That's all right. The point is to recognize that thousands of powerful thoughts, emotions, and ideas are constantly swimming around in your head. All you have to do is dive in to grab them. (Take a closer look at your free-writing exercise. Is there a word, sentence, or subject that you'd like to explore further in your journal? Do it!)

Explore the Real You

Although her grades were good, twelve-year-old Hailey was convinced she didn't have any special talent. She did not appear to excel in athletics, music, or art the way her friends did. Frustrated, Hailey poured out every awful detail of her failures in her journal—like the time she tried out for the softball team and caught a fly ball with her nose. Only when she reread her "crash and burn" entries did Hailey find something to smile about. "I laughed so hard reading my old stuff," she says, "but I also learned some things about myself, too. I discovered that I have a lot of determination. I don't give up on things easily. Also, I have a real passion for writing. My journal showed me I'm not as hopeless as I thought."

"Journaling is a road to self-discovery," says Patrick, who began keeping a journal in the sixth grade. "But more than self-discovery, journaling made me grow. It got me questioning some of the things that everyone accepts 'as is' and wanting to find answers to the 'whys.'" Did you ever wonder where your opinions, values, likes, and dislikes originate? Do 'The Real You' exercise on p. 20. It will encourage you to spend more time thinking about what makes you distinct, from your simplest desires to your deepest beliefs.

Build Confidence and Self-Esteem

Nobody is perfect. We seem to be either "too this" or

The Real You

What's your favorite food? *Macaroni and cheese.*
Why is it your favorite food? *I don't know. It just is.*

We know what we like, but we may not stop to think about *why* we like it. Sure, macaroni and cheese tastes great, but there might be more to it than that. Maybe you also like it because your grandmother has a special recipe or your mom makes it for you when you've had a bad day at school. Try the following exercise. As you answer, work to go beyond the simple explanation "because I do" to stretch for a deeper reason. For instance, you might say, "My favorite color is red because red is vibrant and cheerful like me." If you can't come up with a reason for each response, leave that part of your answer blank and try again later.

My favorite color is: _____

because: _____

My favorite subject in school is: _____

    because: _____

My favorite type of music is: _____

    because: _____

I wish I could: _____

    because _____

I am afraid of: _____

    because: _____

The thing I most admire about myself is: _____

    because: _____

It bothers me when people say: _____

    because: _____

Did you leave several of the "whys" blank? It's all right if you did. Many of us don't give serious thought to the reasons behind our likes, dislikes, attitudes, and values. As you prepare to create your own journal, start thinking about the "whys" in your life. Come up with some of your own questions to answer.

"too that"—too tall or too short, too thin or too fat, too pretty or too ugly. Do kids tease you because you have braces, glasses, freckles, weird hair, or another feature that seems to set you apart from everybody else? At some point in life, most everyone gets teased about something. If you take such negative comments to heart, instead of believing in yourself, it can slowly eat away at your self-confidence and self-esteem. Self-esteem is your belief in your worth as a person. Journaling can help overcome many of these insecurities. The more comfortable you become with yourself in your journal, the more you'll see that you do not need approval from others. You'll discover that who you are on the inside is far more important than the way you look.

Journaling will help smooth away the doubts that you have nothing to contribute to the world, for in your journal your great ideas and unique way of seeing the world will come shining through.

Also, the sense of accomplishment you get from creating a journal will give your confidence a boost. The process of journaling will help smooth away the doubts that you have nothing to contribute to the world, for in your journal your great ideas, sense of humor, compassion for others, artistic talent, and unique way of seeing the world will come shining through. Use your journal to take risks, set goals, and reach for your dreams.

Cope with Challenges

Born in South Korea, Megan was adopted into an American family when she was a baby. At age three, she was diagnosed with autism, a developmental disorder that impairs a person's ability to learn, interact, and communicate with others. In the fifth grade, Megan began journaling not only to improve her writing and communications skills but also to explore her feelings about adoption. "In my younger days, I always felt left out because I was the only child in my class who didn't know her birth mother or father," she says. "Journaling helped me deal with the pain." Now eighteen years old and in college, Megan continues to journal and, once in a while, goes back to review her old entries. "They are a huge reminder that I have made it. A child who was diagnosed with a disease that often makes them an outcast has made it in the 'real world.'"

Research reveals that writing about painful feelings or events can be just as helpful as discussing them with someone. Writing releases strong emotions, such as anger, fear, and sadness. It isn't uncommon to bottle up such emotions because thinking about them can hurt. Yet if we are willing to let them bubble to the surface, we can begin to deal with what is bothering us. Whether you are handling problems at school, a divorce, moving, an illness, the loss of a loved one, or simply the normal trials of growing up, your journal is a safe place for you to release all of the jumbled emotions you may be feeling.

"When I was confused, journaling put me back on track," reveals Gabrielle, a teen who began journaling at age twelve to help cope with severe depression and suicidal thoughts. Severe depression is a mental illness in which someone experiences deep sadness, despair, hopelessness, and worthlessness and may consider suicide. It interferes with a person's ability to participate in normal activities and daily life. "When you write things out, you tend to see things in a different way than when you were originally overwhelmed by your feelings and thoughts," explains Gabrielle, whose parents worked long hours and did not realize the seriousness of her illness. "It doesn't matter that the paper doesn't answer back or give me advice. It's an outlet. When the anger and hatred that comes with depression is directed toward writing and not yourself or the world, you don't really feel like killing yourself anymore."

Self-expression can be a powerful tool. Sometimes, thoughts and feelings you weren't even aware of can flow out of your head and onto the page. Releasing emotions doesn't mean you have to act on them. Just letting them go and being with them is often all you need to do. Remember, even if you regret something you wrote in your journal, don't cross out anything or destroy it. If you must, make a small, dated notation in the margin using a different ink color, but leave the original entry alone.

Although journaling can ease the burden of struggling with a difficult issue, it may not always be enough. If you ever feel overwhelmed by your emotions or unable to deal with a problem, ask for help. Talk to your parents, a teacher, or a school counselor about what you're facing. It may also be necessary to seek assistance from a psychotherapist, a trained and licensed mental-health professional.

Take Your Mood Pulse

Each time you sit down to journal, gauge your current emotional state by asking yourself, "How am I feeling right now?" Pick one word to sum up your mood: "annoyed," "crabby," "dreamy," "giggly," etc. Once you zero in on an emotion, write it at the top corner of your journal. When you finish your entry, take your "mood pulse" again and log it at the bottom of the page. Are you feeling better? Worse? About the same? Focusing in on your emotions as you journal will help you better express your true self.

Improve Your Health

Scientists have found that releasing intense emotions

through writing benefits both mind and body. "Evidence shows the more specific one can be about writing about a painful incident, the better the emotional and health benefits," says psychologist Dr. Ellen Baker, who recommends journaling to many of her patients. In a journal, you can write the things you may not feel comfortable saying to others.

Have you ever been so mad at a friend that you sat down and, in all your fury, wrote a nasty letter? Chances are if you sent the letter you probably regretted doing so the moment it left your hands. Why? Because once we let go of our intense emotions through writing, our stress level drops and we begin to feel better. Stress not only plays a role in our mental well-being but also affects the function of the immune system, the body's ability to fight infection and disease. Writing about painful experiences, and coming to terms with these events in our lives, has been shown to reduce stress and improve the function of the immune system. University of Texas psychology professor Dr. James Pennebaker has been studying the connection between self-expression and health for more than thirty years. "Some of the most important studies have required people to write about emotional upheavals in their lives for three to four days for only twenty minutes a day," he explains. "What we find is that emotional writing has a powerful effect on people's health. They are less likely to go to a doctor for colds, flus, headaches, and other problems." Expressive writing has also been shown to reduce the symptoms of chronic diseases, such as arthritis, asthma, diabetes, and AIDS.

Grow in Your Relationships

A journal can bring you closer to family and friends because when you are writing about the people in your life, you are taking the time to reflect on your relationships. In your journal, you can share your problems, worries, and questions about others, while listening for the answers that echo back to you. Studies have also found that journaling improves social and communication skills—important factors for building and strengthening friendships.

"When I went to high school, I started carrying around a little journal with me in my purse where I would write down random ideas or things I'd overhear," recalls Katie Merz, editor of *Personal Journaling* magazine. "I'd even bring it out at times and ask other people to write in it. I discovered so much about myself and other people by doing this. I realized that sometimes all you have to do to find out more about someone else is to ask. I learned that writing could be a way of connecting with people."

Some people keep a friendship journal, a book that is shared among two or more friends. Each person takes a turn writing in the journal before passing it to the next friend.

Your Personal Timeline

A timeline is a sequential log of major events in history. Between the day of your birth and today, you have been creating your own personal timeline. As you think back, what are some of the most important things that have happened to you? Did you move to a new city? Achieve a hard-fought goal? Gain a brother or sister? Write down seven (or more) of the most defining moments in your life. Include such events as graduations, illnesses, weddings, vacations, births and deaths, special occasions, and achievements. You might also want to include when you met a special person who has had a significant influence on you.

On a piece of paper, draw a vertical line. Put your name and birth date at the top of the line. Below your birth date begin drawing "branches" from the vertical line, one branch for each significant happening in your life. Going in chronological order from earliest to most recent, write the date on the left side of the line and the event on the right. (You can follow the sample timeline at the right.) Keep your timeline in your journal. As important happenings occur, add them so that you can see the turning points that have shaped the person you are today.

Nathan's Timeline

9/07/93	I was born.
9/07/98	First day of kindergarten (on my birthday). Met Ms. Wick, my favorite teacher.
4/12/99	My sister, Lindsay, was born (I was hoping for a brother).
5/00	Fell off my scooter and broke my leg.
4/01	Went to Disneyland for a week with my family. I love California!
12/02	Moved to Colorado.
2/03	Grandpa died & grandma came to live with us.
7/03	First day of soccer camp. I want to be an MLS soccer player!

Eleven-year-old Marie and her mom, Debra, keep a mother-daughter friendship journal. In it, they write about their activities, pose questions to one another, and swap jokes. "I wanted a way for Marie and I to talk about some of the things she wouldn't otherwise be able to tell me," explains Debra. "It's a good outlet for her to express herself and ask me questions when she wants to. Also, I wanted her to have a record of her childhood and the memories we made together."

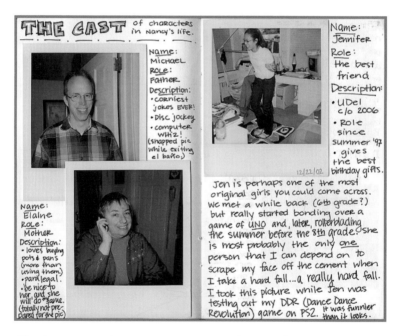

Sharing a journal is a great way to get closer to friends and family. Like the entry from book #920 of the 1,000 Journals Project (above), you can describe your own 'cast' of writers and even include photos.

Eleven-year-old Marie and her mom, Debra, keep a mother-daughter friendship journal. In it, they write about their activities, pose questions to one another, and swap jokes.

Chart Your History

Day by day, as you add to it, your journal connects the dots to reveal your life. If you choose, you can revisit the past anytime you want. Explore your finest accomplishments and biggest mistakes. Recall quiet moments and major milestones. You may even want to make your own personal timeline.

If you decide to read your old journal entries, you might be surprised to find how much you have grown and changed, even after just a few months. "When I go back through my journal, I'm amazed at how upset I got over something that's so unimportant now," says Ben, age fourteen. "But it was a major deal at the time, and I usually learned something from it." Yesterday helped shape the person you are today, and today will affect who you become tomorrow. So use your journal to preserve the past, record the present, and plan for the future.

Three

Time Travel

"T he little clouds spread far. They looked like white scrambled eggs," aviation pioneer Amelia Earhart scrawled in her logbook on June 2, 1937, as her Lockheed Electra soared over Puerto Rico. Just one day before, Earhart and her navigator, Fred Noonan, had taken off from Miami, Florida, on a daring round-the-world flight. Throughout her voyage, Earhart transmitted her journal notes back to the United States via cable, telephone, and mail. In one entry, she described taking off from a rain-soaked runway in Calcutta, India, as "precarious, perhaps as risky as any we had. The plane clung for what seemed like ages to the heavy, sticky soil before the wheels finally lifted, and we cleared with nothing at all to spare the fringe of trees at the airdrome's edge."

Once Earhart returned, her journal entries were to be compiled for a book heralding her achievement, to be called *World Flight*. The day before she left Lae, New Guinea, on the final leg of her trip home, Amelia made one last, haunting entry:

> "Not much more than a month ago I was on the other shore of the Pacific, looking westward. This evening, I looked eastward over the Pacific. In those fast-moving days which have intervened, the whole width of the world has passed between us—except this broad ocean. I shall be glad when we have the hazards of its navigation behind us."

But it was not to be. On July 2, 1937, Earhart and Noonan took off from New Guinea to fly a 2,556-mile (4,112-kilometer) route over the Pacific Ocean never before traveled by plane. They planned to land and refuel at Howland Island, a tiny dot less than three-quarters of a square mile (2 square kilometers) in the central Pacific. The pair never made it. Earhart's plane vanished without a trace over the ocean. The plane may have had mechanical problems, run out of fuel, or drifted off course. No one knows what went wrong, but most experts conclude the plane probably crashed into the Pacific. After her disappearance, Earhart's husband, publisher

George Putnam, printed his wife's journal and letters just as they had planned. The title of the book, however, was changed from *World Flight* to *Last Flight.*

Published historical journals, like Amelia Earhart's, give us a rare chance to view the world through the eyes of an extraordinary human being. Historians refer to such accounts as primary sources because they offer a glimpse into an important place, event, or time from a personal point of view. Photographs, drawings, and letters are also primary sources. A primary source gives us insight into the past as only someone who has been there can do. It may reveal interesting facts about a culture, or show us the challenges and dreams of a people. It may reveal the tragedies of humanity, teaching us valuable lessons we can carry into the future.

Some of history's most noted artists, poets, writers, politicians, explorers, inventors, religious leaders, and even criminals have kept journals. Historical journals open a window in time. We cannot trek across the rugged American West with explorers Meriwether Lewis and William Clark. We cannot hear President Abraham Lincoln discuss how the division of

Some of history's most noted artists, poets, writers, politicians, explorers, inventors, religious leaders, and even criminals have kept journals.

his country over slavery deeply troubled him. We cannot sit in the cockpit beside aviation pioneer Amelia Earhart on her ill-fated flight around the world. But we can read their amazing journals. Their words can make us feel as if we were there at the very moment they put pen to paper.

Journaling Pioneer

The diary of Englishman Samuel Pepys (1633–1703), an administrator for the British navy, was one of the first modern journals ever to be published (part of the journal was printed in 1825, and a complete eleven-volume edition was published in the 1970s). From 1660 to 1669, Pepys chronicled his life in London. He scribbled his entries in a type of shorthand called tachygraphy, used by clerks and lawyers of his day.

While Pepys's journal is filled with typical news about his health, work, and social life, it also offers a unique look at several major events of the seventeenth century. In the mid-1660s, the last major outbreak of the bubonic plague in England killed seventy thousand people. In his diary, Pepys wrote about the horrors of the plague, called the Black Death, which took the life of his aunt and physician. Soon after, Pepys would witness the worst fire in London's history. On the morning of September 2, 1666, a fire began in a bakery near the Thames River. Fanned by gusty winds, wooden structures built too closely together, and garbage in the streets, flames raced quickly through the heart of the city.

"We stayed till, it being darkish, we saw the fire as only one entire arch of fire from this to the other side of the bridge, and in a bow up the hill, for an arch of above a mile long. It made me weep to see it. The churches, houses, and all on fire and flaming at once, and a horrid noise the flames made, and the cracking of houses at their ruine."

—Samuel Pepys, September 2, 1666

Pepys described being overcome by the "shower of Firedrops" that consumed two-thirds of the city "in a most horrid malicious bloody flame, not like the fine flame of an ordinary fire." Pepys narrowly missed losing his own home in the Great Fire of London, which burned for five days and destroyed more than thirteen thousand homes and ninety churches.

Eyestrain caused Pepys to give up regular journaling in 1669, but his adventures were far from over. In 1679, the year he was elected to Parliament, Pepys was accused of betraying his country and selling British naval secrets to the French. Although the charges were later dropped,

Pepys was imprisoned for six weeks in the Tower of London. Until his death, Pepys continued to journal now and then, though these later works were not as lengthy or as detailed as those he wrote in the 1660s.

Renaissance Man

Italian artist and scientist Leonardo da Vinci (1452–1519) carried notebooks with him wherever he went, sketching pictures to accompany his brilliant observations on science, art, nature, architecture, flight, and philosophy. His journals reveal a genius with amazing insight into the future. Leonardo's detailed drawings of the human body helped doctors understand the human circulatory system and paved the way to better surgical techniques. He was a pioneer in the field of hydraulics, the study of fluids in motion and at rest. He even designed an underwater diving suit. Leonardo also spent many hours watching and drawing the movement of birds, a fascination that led to the anticipation of flying machines and the parachute.

Children of War

In 1933, the year Adolph Hitler was appointed chancellor of Germany, four-year-old Anne Frank and her family fled to Holland. The Franks were Jewish, and Hitler's Nazi party was leading a campaign of racial persecution against the

Jewish people. Hitler inaccurately blamed Germany's unemployment, poverty, and economic problems on the Jews. Under his rule, Jews were not allowed to teach in schools, practice law or medicine, or hold public office. Most were stripped of their businesses and property. Jewish children were forbidden to go to German schools. Jewish synagogues were burned. As part of Hitler's "final solution," Jews were rounded up by the thousands and shipped to concentration camps. At the camps, those who were not gassed or shot to death lived in wretched conditions until they died of disease or starvation.

In Amsterdam, Anne Frank's early childhood was peaceful, filled with schoolwork, friends, and parties. However, everything changed in 1940 when Hitler's army invaded Holland. The Nazi police, known as the Gestapo, began rounding up Jews for deportation to concentration camps. In the meantime, Anne's father, Otto, made plans to hide his wife and two daughters in the attic of his office building. On July 6, 1942, with World War II in full swing, Anne climbed up a hidden staircase in the back of her father's office and entered "the secret annex." She brought with her only a few things, including the diary her parents had recently given her for her thirteenth birthday. For the next two years, Anne would share her innermost thoughts with the journal she fondly called Kitty.

Wednesday, January 13, 1943

Dearest Kitty,

Terrible things are happening outside. At any time of night and day, poor helpless people are being dragged out of their homes... Families are torn apart; men, women, and children are separated. Children come home from school to find their parents have disappeared... Everyone is scared... the entire world is at war, and even though the Allies are doing better, the end is nowhere in sight. As for us, we're quite fortunate. Luckier than millions of people. It's quiet and safe here, and we're using our money to buy food... I could spend hours telling you about the suffering the war has brought, but I'd only make myself more miserable. All we can do is wait, as calmly as possible, for it to end. Jews and Christians alike are waiting, the whole world is waiting, and many are waiting for death.

Yours, Anne

In the spring of 1944, Anne began revising her diary in the hopes of publishing a book once the war ended. "I want to go on living even after my death!" she wrote. "And that's why I'm so grateful to God for having given me this gift, which I can use to develop myself and to express all that's inside me! When I write I can shake off all my cares. My sorrow disappears, my spirits are revived!"

"I want to go on living even after my death! I'm so grateful to God for having given me this gift, which I can use to develop myself and to express all that's inside me!"

On August 4, 1944, on a tip from a Dutch informer, the Gestapo raided the secret annex. While looting the annex for money and valuables, the police dumped the contents of Otto Frank's briefcase on the floor, which included Anne's original diary and hundreds of loose pages she'd written. The Franks and the other residents of the attic were arrested. As her family was taken away, Anne was forced to leave her precious journals behind. The Franks were part of the last shipment of Jews sent out of Holland bound for Auschwitz, a concentration camp in Poland. On the train platform at Auschwitz, men and women were separated. Otto Frank never saw his wife or daughters again. That winter, Anne's mother died of illness. Anne and her sixteen-year-old sister, Margot, were moved to Bergen-Belsen camp in Germany. In March 1945, two months before Germany officially surrendered to the Allies and a few days after the death of her sister, Anne Frank died of typhus. She was not yet sixteen years old.

Anne's father managed to survive the brutal conditions at Auschwitz. Upon returning to Holland after the war, he learned that two secretaries who had helped hide his family had

Living Legacy

Jacob, age fourteen, was startled to read an on-line news story reporting that, every day, nearly one thousand whales, dolphins, and porpoises around the world drown after getting tangled in fishing gear. Jacob, who loves visiting the ocean, printed out the article and stuck it in his journal. The issue fueled his desire to learn more about ocean preservation. After doing a little research, Jacob discovered there were some simple steps his family could take to help protect marine life, such as not using chlorine bleach, fertilizers, or other toxic chemicals that would end up polluting local streams and rivers.

Watch the evening news, read a newspaper, or go on-line tonight and find a news story that touches you.

Write a paragraph describing the issue as if you were explaining it to someone who knew nothing about it. As you write, ask yourself these questions:

- How did this issue or problem occur?
- What are some ways it might be solved?
- Is there anything I can do, right now, to make a difference?

You may not be able to solve serious global issues like disease, hunger, or pollution. Yet, you might find—like Jacob, who is considering a career in marine biology—that a simple shift in habit or attitude could make a world of difference.

rescued Anne's original diary, along with more than three hundred loose pages she'd written. In 1947, he published his daughter's journal. In the years following World War II, *Anne Frank: The Diary of a Young Girl* would speak for the more than six million Jews, including a million children, who died at the hands of the Nazis. To date, twenty-five million copies of Anne's diary have been published in sixty languages. Anne Frank did, indeed, get her wish, for she continues to live on long after her death.

Your Place in History

Minute by minute, history is being made and you are a living, breathing part of it. Consider some of the major news stories of the past decade: the September 11th, 2001, terrorist attacks on the World Trade Center and the Pentagon, the wars in Iraq and Afghanistan, the *Columbia* space shuttle disaster. What would you have written had you kept a journal during these times?

History has a way of slowly wrapping itself around us. It affects our opinions, beliefs, ideals, and lifestyle. Take a moment to reflect on the major news stories of today. Are you passionate about a certain topic, perhaps rain-forest destruction, global warming, or the protection of endangered species? Whatever is happening in the world—whether it is halfway around the planet or in your own backyard—share your feelings about it in your journal.

"History never looks like history when you are living through it," pointed out writer John Gardner. "It looks confusing and messy, and it always feels uncomfortable." It may not be easy discussing perplexing issues, senseless events, or tragedy in your journal. Even so, expressing your views, questions, impressions, ideas, fears, and feelings

"History never looks like history when you are living through it."

about these things better connects you with the world. As you become more aware and informed, you might change your way of thinking, get involved in a cause, encourage others to make a difference, or stumble upon a future career. You might even find your place in history.

Four

Write Now!

I n your journal, you have complete creative control. You are free to write, type, sketch, paint, or collage anything you want. Even so, there may be some subjects you don't feel comfortable discussing. It's all right to have some topics that are taboo, or off-limits, for journaling. Just be certain that you are the one who determines this and not someone else. On p. 48, try the exercise Dr. Kate Hays, psychologist and journaler, uses to get people thinking about the important issues in their lives.

Don't get discouraged if you find it tough to actually begin writing. An empty sheet of white paper or a blinking cursor

Fair or Forbidden?

Are there subjects you want to make sure you cover in your journal? Are there some you definitely don't want to discuss? Take a moment to think it over, then copy the following sentences and fill in the blanks (make a longer list, if you need to):

In my journal, I can write about: _____

_____

_____

In my journal, I cannot write about: _____

_____

_____

"Ask yourself why you are not able to write about these things," prompts psychologist Dr. Kate Hays. "Are they too painful? Would you have to deal with something you aren't yet prepared to face? Someone with an eating disorder might say, 'I cannot write down what I eat during the day,' because it might mean comparing what she eats to what others her age are eating. It would mean coming to terms with the fact that she isn't taking in enough food, and she might not be ready to do that just yet."

Now, explore one more thought:

In my journal, I would be able to write about: _____

_____

_____

if only: _____

_____

_____

Don't put any pressure on yourself to write about your taboo topics. When it is the right time to share them in your journal, you will instinctively know it.

on a computer screen can be scary, at first. To help yourself feel more at ease, pretend you are writing a letter to a friend. Tell your journal about your likes, dislikes, friends, interests, etc. Write a poem or draw a cartoon. The more you journal, the easier it will become to tap into your thoughts, emotions, and impressions. Gradually, what to say and how to say it will start to flow naturally.

And Number One Is...

Anytime you wrestle with writer's block, break it with a Top 10 list. Name your ten favorite foods or the ten least favorite. How about your Top 10 movies, jokes, celebrities, sports heroes, or places you want to travel to someday? What are your ten best qualities, career choices, goals, best (and worst) haircuts? You can make a Top 10 list for just about anything, from your brother's most disgusting habits to your favorite songs.

Quiet, Please!

While you are journaling, it's important that you not be interrupted. Look for a quiet spot where you won't be distracted. If you choose to journal in your bedroom, you might make a "Do Not Disturb" sign to put on your door. You don't always have to journal at the same time in the same place. Go outside and sit under a tree. Find a comfy couch in the library. A change of scenery can be inspiring.

You can journal at any time of the day or night. Many people like to sit down with their journals at the end of the day, right before bedtime, but the choice is yours. If you prefer to make an entry first thing in the morning or right after you get home from school, that's all right, too. You may find it helpful to write at around the same time each day.

You're free to write in your journal as little or as often as you want. A journal is a reflection of your life, so when you choose to add to it is completely up to you. Some people write something, no matter how little, each day. Many make an entry only once or twice a week. Others carry a small notebook with them wherever they go so they can make notations whenever interesting things occur. If you let a couple of weeks or even a month go by without writing, don't let that stop you from picking up your journal again. Nobody is keeping score.

If you let a couple of weeks or even a month go by without writing, don't let that stop you from picking up your journal again.

Keep Out! (or Maybe Not)

Some people would never dream of letting anyone read their journal, while others are open about revealing their entries. Many people keep a friendship journal, along with a personal journal that is strictly for their eyes alone. In a personal journal, privacy is an essential ingredient because in order to freely explore yourself, you have to feel safe from judgment. It is hard to be completely truthful if, in the back of your mind, you think that someone is going to read your words. After you've made an entry, it's all right to show it to someone you trust. However, the choice must be yours to make.

To ensure privacy, you may want to take a few security measures to protect your journal. Find a secret place to hide your journal: deep in a drawer, in a pillowcase, in your closet, or in a locked trunk or box. Some journal books have built-in security devices, such as a sturdy key or a voice-recognition password. Another kind of journal comes with a special pen and an ultraviolet, or black, light. Any words written with the pen are invisible and cannot be read until placed under the black light. Writer Beatrix Potter, author of *Peter Rabbit,* wrote her diary entries using a secret code she devised. For the computer, many journaling software programs and on-line journaling Web sites feature password-protected entry so that only you can log on.

No matter how careful you are, no security method is foolproof. Ultimately, you will have to trust those around you. If you like, tell your family members you are keeping a journal. Ask that they respect your privacy and not read it without your consent. It is absolutely critical that your friends and family members comply with your wishes.

Anne Frank used to put her diary in her father's briefcase at night for safekeeping. "I promised her never to look at it," Otto Frank once said in an interview. "I never did."

If someone does read your journal, don't panic. You may be angry, disappointed, or embarrassed. Perhaps the person who saw your journal wants to confront you about something you wrote. Make it clear that you will not discuss any of your entries. Sometimes, a parent may sneak a peek at a journal out of concern for a child with failing grades, with questionable friends, or who may be engaged in criminal activity. While these worries are understandable, they do not justify breaking a trust. You do not need to apologize, explain, or feel bad about anything you have written. Most important, don't let it discourage you from journaling. Reexamine your security measures, make changes if necessary, and begin again.

You do not need to apologize, explain, or feel bad about anything you have written.

Choosing a Journal

Think about how you like to express yourself. Do you prefer the computer to a pen? Maybe you like calligraphy, sketching, painting, or taking photographs. Perhaps you like to sing, play an instrument, or get in front of the camera. Time spent with your journal should be something you look forward to, so choose a journal that lets you express yourself in a satisfying way.

In the United States, retailers sell more than ten million blank journals every year. You'll find a wide selection of journals and sketchbooks in various sizes, styles, and colors at your local bookstore and art- or office-supply store. Some journals have specialty paper, many feature fancy leather or beaded covers, while others are devoted to themes, such as dreams, pets, and hobbies. Look for a journal that is at least 6 inches by 9 inches so you'll have plenty of room to write and draw. If you plan on including lots of photos and other mementos in your journal, consider a scrapbook (they are typically 8 inches by 11 inches or 12 inches by 12 inches). Decorative papers designed just for scrapbooks are sturdy enough to hold photos, news or magazine articles, concert programs, ticket stubs, invitations, greeting cards, postcards, award certificates—you name it!

You can buy a bound journal, or you can make one your-self. A three-ring binder filled with standard lined notebook paper is an affordable and flexible journal. You can also divide your journal into sections, if you want. A favorite pen will work just fine for making entries.

Allow your creative side to blossom. Add drawings, sketches, cartoons, comics, or doodles (if you decide to paint with watercolor or acrylics, make sure you choose a heavy-bond paper to handle the medium). Look to art-supply, craft, and scrapbooking stores for inventive ideas to spruce up your journal, such as specialty papers, paints, stickers, stamps, and stencils. Don't think you are a talented artist? You are! Art is a form of individual expression, which means we *all* have the ability to do it. Your drawings won't be like anyone else's, and that's the way it should be. Ready to give it a try? Tackle the drawing exercise below. If you've never explored your artistic side, try doing so at least once a week in your journal.

From the Heart

In the early 1900s, the paintings of artists such as Paul Cézanne, Georges Braque, and Pablo Picasso emphasized emotion, feeling, and color over traditional shape and form—a style of painting that became known as the cubist movement. Today, art historians view cubism as one of the most powerful influences on twentieth-century art, because it freed artists to express their own individual style.

Pick a word from the list below and draw how it makes you feel. Don't think about it. Don't ask anyone's opinion. Take a tip from the cubists, and let your heart guide you.

hunger	*float*	*globule*
chatterbox	*winter*	*lonely*
love	*whisper*	*greed*
swift	*invisible*	*shiver*

Anytime you come across a new, interesting, or descriptive word, trying sketching in your journal how it makes you feel.

For those who want to journal on their computer, most journaling and scrapbooking software programs feature cool borders, backgrounds, fonts, balloon quotes, clip art, and graphics, along with password protection. Take digital photos of friends, family, and special events to plug into your computer journal or print out for your paper journal. Some programs allow you to download your favorite pictures or songs from the Web. You can also keep a web diary on the Internet.

On-line journaling took off in the mid-1990s with the rise of personal Web sites. Today, thousands of people keep on-line diaries, including celebrities like Avril Lavigne, William Shatner, Kylie Minogue, Wil Wheaton, Jeff Bridges, Alyssa Milano, and Al Roker. Some on-line journaling Web sites are free, but many charge a small fee. Typically, you will have several security options. You can keep your journal completely private, make it available only to those you know via password, or allow it to be viewed by anyone. You may have heard on-line journals being referred to as web logs—or "blogs" for short—but the two are not the same. A web log is someone's personal commentary about sites or information on the worldwide web, whereas an on-line journal or diary is a personal account of someone's life. Although a blog and a web journal are different, the lines are beginning to blur because more people are using the terms interchangeably. If you want to journal on-line, first get approval from your parents. Choose a site geared for young people, and never give out your real name, address, or phone number to *anyone* on-line.

Seventeen-year-old Lauren Dado, who lives near Manila in the Philippines, has been keeping a journal on the Internet since she was ten years old. Lauren, who calls her journal *The Protagonist,* began recording her life on-line because, "it seemed like a different and more interesting way of expressing myself." Occasionally, Lauren password-protects her more personal notes, but most of her entries are available for anyone who logs on to read. "I love the anonymity the Internet gives me," she explains. "It makes me feel more comfortable about being open about myself. Writing in my on-line journal also makes me feel less alone when I'm facing certain difficulties and problems." Her advice for web journalers: "Be yourself. You'll be surprised at the number of people all over the world who can relate to you. On the Internet, it's just impossible not to meet someone who can understand you."

Lauren Dado's On-Line Journal Entry   *December 22, 1996*

Everybody's excited about Christmas. My friends are making New Year's Resolutions already. The main resolution I would want to make is to stop pretending. I pretend a lot. I pretend I'm a girl from Beverly Hills… I pretend because I want to mix in.

My New Year's Resolutions: (don't laugh, for some may sound silly)

1. Stop that pretending business. Sometimes I feel dumb when I pretend and sometimes I don't like it. Sometimes I like it too. It makes me feel like I'm a different person. It's all too personal so I'm not going to write it here.

2. Improve my writing. I mean, I think I'm a great writer. But I guess my stories would need more. Know what I'm saying?

*3. I've really got this bad habbit of mine. *blush* I keep biting my nails. I want to stop but I can't. Duh. I know it's stupid and childish.*

4. Stop acting as if I'm older!!! That's one of my problems too. I pretend I'm 17 or something. Anything to shake off the feeling that I'm 10. I hate being 10. I don't like being 10. 10 is a childish age for me. You're always being regarded as childish and weird. But this is one thing that I keep in mind: I'm an extraordinary 10-year-old. No, I'm not bragging about this fact, but how many 10-year-olds write? Well, I guess I was just a born writer. I've been writing since I was four and I can't stop.

5. Do something about my hair and face! Sometimes, I don't think I'm pretty enough or my hair always flies to Mars (my expression) so I really have to do something.

Camcorders and audio tape recorders also make excellent journals because they capture real life as it happens. Take a camcorder with you when you go to the mall, to an amusement park, or on vacation. Make a family video journal, and interview your parents, brothers, sisters, and grandparents about their lives. Chances are you'll hear some incredible stories and learn some fascinating facts about your family.

Camcorders and audio tape recorders also make excellent journals because they capture real life as it happens.

Feel free to experiment with the various journaling formats we've explored, adding your own twists and ideas. If ever you find something isn't working for you in your journal, don't be afraid to change it. Try new pens or papers, or go for a completely different format. Craft a journal you love, and you will find yourself coming back to it again and again.

It may be that one, two, or more kinds of journals spark your interest. Keeping several journals is not an uncommon practice. Jessica Wilber, who at age fourteen wrote the book *Totally Private and Personal Journaling Ideas for Girls and Young Women,* keeps a number of journals: a computer journal; a three-ring binder for regular journal entries and dreams; another binder for drawings, poetry, story ideas, and song lyrics; and a little notebook she carries around with her at all times to write down her spontaneous thoughts.

If you're a beginner, you might want to start with a main journal and a small pad or spiral notebook that you can take with you. Or try a theme journal devoted to a particular topic such as dreams, sports, family, artwork, fiction, poetry, or travel. "What do you love? Dedicate a journal to it," encourages Katie Merz, editor of *Personal Journaling* magazine. "Do you have a favorite show, band, actor, entertainer, hobby, game, etc.? Start writing down all the things you love about it. Get others to share what they love about it, too, inside its pages. Loosen up about what you think a journal should look like and make it what you WANT it to be."

Come to Your Senses

You can breathe life into your journal by using your five senses to their full potential. "If you tell what you see, hear, touch, smell, and taste as you write, you will be immersed in the place you are describing and realize you have quite a lot to write about," says Sheila Bender, publisher of the on-line magazine WritingItReal.com. "Keep yourself from the temptation to summarize with words like 'beautiful,' 'horrible,' and 'nice,' and you will find that you are more interested in what you have to write in your journal." Instead of writing, "lunch was awful," try using your senses to explain what you mean in detail. You might say, "the chicken dumplings bobbed like forgotten golf balls in a chunky swamp of green mystery gravy." Next time you go somewhere new, sit down and write five sentences to describe your surroundings, one for each of your senses.

In the end, a journal is everything that is you—your desires, fears, hopes, problems, goals, loves, passions, obstacles, beliefs, and traditions. It is the sand between your toes and the raindrops on your forehead. It is a fight with a friend and a hundred "I'm sorry's." It is moments of triumph and tear-stained pages. You are its heart, and it is your soul. Or is it the other way around? You decide.

Five

A Thirty-Day Journal

The following month-long journal is designed to let you slowly dip your toes into the sea of journaling. By the time you're finished, you will be ready to plunge in on your own. Don't worry if you miss one, two, or even seven days. Go at your own pace. Once you begin journaling on your own, return to this chapter whenever you need an idea to boost your creativity. Be sure to date every entry and, if you want, take your mood pulse when you begin and again when you finish. One final tip: Before you start each journaling session, spend a few minutes winding down. Close your eyes, take a few deep breaths, and clear your mind of all outside distractions. You are now ready to journal!

Day One: Create a title page that reflects who you are through collage, drawing, painting, or photos. Add an inspirational quote, religious verse, or poem if it feels right. Give your journal a name if you'd like, just as Anne Frank did.

Day Two: Write a letter introducing yourself to your journal. Describe what you look like, your favorite foods, activities, music, and TV shows. Include details about your family, pets, and friends. Glue in a photo, or draw a self-portrait. Did you remember to date your entry?

Day Three: Where is your favorite place in the world? Did you go there on a family trip or is it so close you can go there anytime you want? Describe how it makes you feel to be in your favorite spot: peaceful, content, free, alive, etc. Tell your journal why you love it so.

Day Four: Pretend you are a fly on your wall. Describe your room using as many senses as you can: What does it smell like? Sound like? Feel like? Draw a map of your room, too.

Day Five: Write or draw the best thing about being your present age. Now write or draw what is the worst thing about being your age. Are you taking your mood pulse regularly?

Day Six: Draw or write about anything you want today, but do it with your opposite hand. Do you find that you think differently? Write shorter sentences? Draw better or worse than you expected?

Day Seven: Finish this sentence: The one thing no one knows about me is _____. Why is this such a secret? What would happen if people find out about the "real you?"

Day Eight: A simile is comparing one thing to another, often using the words "like" or "as" to do so. For instance, the phrase "her voice grated on me like an angry parakeet" uses simile. A metaphor refers to one thing as if it were another: "His eyes were two stars in a moonless sky." Using simile and metaphor, describe each of these people in a few sentences: a teacher, a friend, a family member, yourself.

Day Nine: What was your birth or adoption like? Interview your mom and dad, grandparents, and older brothers and sisters to find out what happened the day you came into their lives. Write the full story in your journal. Include your baby picture, if possible.

Day Ten: What is the most embarrassing thing that has ever happened to you? Write and draw the story with as much detail as possible (use simile and metaphor). What did you learn from the experience? Take your mood pulse.

Day Eleven: No words today. In your journal, draw how you feel at this very moment. Remember, your picture doesn't have to be anything recognizable. It's merely a reflection of your mood, so make squiggles, squares, and funky doodles or scribble using only one color, if you want. Do your thing.

Day Twelve: Write in your journal about your most memorable holiday. It can be a good experience or a bad one. Was it last Halloween? Two Christmases ago? A special Valentine's Day? What made the day so wonderful or so disastrous?

Day Thirteen: A hero is someone you look up to as a role model. He or she is a person who makes an impact on your life, perhaps challenging you to improve and be your best self. Who is your hero, and why?

Day Fourteen: Pretend you are giving advice to someone who is a year younger than you. Finish this sentence: *If I had it to do over again, I would definitely not _____*. Explain why you would behave differently, and describe what you learned from the experience. Peek ahead at tomorrow's exercise so you can prepare.

Day Fifteen: Take your journal with you wherever you go today (you can take a small pad and pen, if you'd rather not lug a large journal around). Write down interesting things you overhear, ideas that come to you, and impressions of your surroundings. Use all five of your senses: sight, smell, sound, taste, and touch. At the end of the day, write in your journal what it was like having your senses "on alert" all day.

Day Sixteen: Compose a letter to someone you know and write the things you've never been able to say out loud. Don't worry—you won't be sending it. You might write to a grandparent that has passed away, a friend you no longer have, or a boy or girlfriend you wished you did have. If it's too difficult to put your feelings into words, then draw a picture, take a photo, or create a collage. Take your mood pulse before and after you journal.

Day Seventeen: Imagine what it would be like to have a superpower. What if you could fly across the galaxy, talk to your cat, or cook hot dogs with your laser-beam eyes? What super-power would you choose and why? Draw yourself wearing your superhero costume.

Day Eighteen: What is the worst gift anyone ever gave you? What is the best gift? Explain. Where are the gifts now?

Day Nineteen: Make a list of ten words that describe your character (no sentences, just a list).

You might use adjectives, like caring, outspoken, messy, impatient, smart, silly, or compassionate. Read over your list, and reflect on why you chose the words that you did. Make another list of ten character traits that you would like to have.

Day Twenty: Think about how you feel regarding issues such as religion, censorship, the death penalty, discrimination, and the environment. Make two lists—one list of the things you believe in and the other of the things you don't believe in.

Day Twenty-One: There is a black hole in the middle of your bedroom, which can take you back to any place and time in history. Where would you choose to go and why? Who would you meet? Would you dare to change history, if you could?

Day Twenty-Two: What is the scariest thing that has ever happened to you? Was it a bike accident, illness, or broken leg? Write down what happened, who helped you through your devastating experience, and what you learned from it.

Day Twenty-Three: Imagine you are a piece of furniture in your parents' or grandparents' house, and tell your story. What has your life been like? What do you hold? What have you witnessed? What do you long to see?

Day Twenty-Four: Be your own fortuneteller and gaze into your crystal ball. What do you see yourself doing five years from now? Ten years? Twenty years? How do you think the world will be different in the future?

Day Twenty-Five: Lie on your bed, and listen to your favorite song. Now, play the song again, only this time draw in your journal how it makes you feel. No words, just pictures.

Day Twenty-Six: Imagine you are a newspaper reporter, and interview a friend or family member about his or her life. Find out about that person's history, interests, and goals. Write his or her story in your journal, and give it an interesting headline.

Day Twenty-Seven: Create an invention the world needs. How would it work? How would it change the planet? Do you think it might ever become reality? Why or why not?

Day Twenty-Eight: Write down three goals you would like to achieve in the next six months (be realistic). What will you need to do to achieve them? Map out a weekly plan to help you reach your goals. Once you begin journaling on your own, you can keep track of your progress. When you meet these goals, set three more!

Day Twenty-Nine: Describe a vivid dream you had recently. Where were you? What happened? How did the dream end? Dreams are symbolic representations of issues and experiences we are dealing with in our waking lives. What do you think your dream might be trying to communicate to you?

Day Thirty: As you near the end of your month-long quest, take this opportunity to review your journal. What are the topics you wished you would have covered? What changes would you like to make? Do you want to add more photos? Switch pens? Get a bigger or smaller journal? Whatever you want to fix, write about it. Then do it!

Glossary

- free writing: writing whatever comes to one's mind without censoring, editing, or revising what flows onto the page; also called free-association writing or stream-of-consciousness writing

- historical journal: a published personal journal written by a notable or famous person

- journal: a personal record of someone's thoughts, feelings, goals, impressions, and life experiences; also called a diary

- primary sources: journals, letters, drawings, photographs, and other materials that offer a look at historical events, places, and times from a personal point of view

psychotherapist: a licensed mental-health professional, such as a psychiatrist or psychologist

self-esteem: someone's belief in his/her own value and worth as a person

timeline: a chronological record of significant events

web journal: a journal kept on the Internet that may or may not be available for the public to read; also called a web diary

web log: an on-line commentary about Web sites or information found on the Internet; called a "blog" for short

writer's block: a term used to express the inability to begin writing or to think of something interesting or worthwhile to write about

writing prompt: a question, thought, or idea about a particular topic used to encourage someone to start writing; writing prompts are often helpful in breaking writer's block

Further Resources

Books

Capacchione, Lucia. *The Creative Journal for Teens: Making Friends With Yourself.* 2nd edition. Franklin Lakes, NJ: New Page Books, 2001.

Check, Laura. *Almost Instant Scrapbooks.* Charlotte, Vt.: Williamson Publishing, 2003.

Filipovic, Zlata. *Zlata's Diary: A Child's Life in Sarajevo.* New York: Viking, 1995.

Frank, Anne. *Anne Frank: The Diary of a Young Girl (The Definitive Edition).* New York: Bantam Books, 1997.

Madden, Kerry. *Writing Smarts: A Girl's Guide to Writing Great Poetry, Stories, School Reports, and More!* Middleton, Wis.: American Girl Publishers, 2002.

Mirriam-Goldberg, Caryn. *Write Where You Are: How to Use Writing to Make Sense of Your Life.* Minneapolis, Minn.: Free Spirit Publishing, 1999.

CD-ROM

Diary Maker (MAC/WIN), Scholastic, Inc. Panasonic Interactive Media Co., 1997. (This may be available in your local library).

It's My Diary (MAC/WIN), JournalTek Software, 2002.

LifeJournal (WIN), Chronicle Software Co., 2001.

Online Sites and Organizations

Diarist.net
www.diarist.net
At this site—the first on the Internet devoted to on-line journaling—you can learn the basics of keeping a web diary. Get ideas to beat writer's block, take a writer's survey, and link to celebrity blogs and journals. Diarist.net is home to the Diarist Awards, honors given by and for web diarists to those with outstanding on-line journals.

Inspired To Journal
www.inspiredtojournal.com
Read articles about journaling, find journaling books, or enter a writing contest at this Web site geared to journalers of all

ages. Get motivational quotes to spice up your journal. Click on "snippets" for a selection of helpful writing prompts.

World Kids Network, Inc.
c/o WAN 2700 NE Andersen Rd., #D-32
Vancouver, WA 98661
www.worldkids.net/tkwc
World Kids Network is a nonprofit organization that promotes the advancement of Internet education among children. At the site, you can create your own home page, join an on-line writers or artists club, or write for an "e-zine" (an on-line magazine).

WritingFix.com
www.writingfix.com
Get writing prompts, play writing games, and enter on-line publishing contests at this site sponsored by the National Writing Project, a nonprofit organization devoted to improving writing in schools across the United States, and the Northern Nevada Writing Project.

Index

About the Author

Trudi Strain Trueit is an award-winning television news reporter and freelance writer who has journaled most of her life. As a teen, she wrote a column for her local newspaper. Her love of writing and storytelling led to a college degree in broadcast journalism and a career in television news. Trudi has contributed stories to ABC News, CBS News, and CNN and was recognized for her medical and health reporting by United Press International and the Society of Professional Journalists.

Her other titles in the *Life Balance* series include *Eating Disorders, ADHD,* and *Dreams and Sleep.* Also a television weather forecaster, she has written more than fifteen books for Scholastic Press on weather, nature, and wildlife. Trudi makes her home in Everett, Washington, with her husband, Bill.

Personal journal excerpt p. 17 used by permission from David Mas Masumoto.

Excerpt pp. 33-34 from *Last Flight* by Amelia Earhart, originally published in 1937 by Harcourt Brace & Company; republished in 1988 by Crown Publishers, a division of Random House.

Excerpt p. 37 reprinted from *The Shorter Pepys: From the Diary of Samuel Pepys,* edited by Robert Latham, University of California Press, 1985. Every reasonable effort has been made to locate the copyright owner of this work. If you identify yourself as the copyright owner please contact Franklin Watts, an imprint of Scholastic Library Publishing.

Excerpt pp. 57-58 used by permission from Lauren Dado, 2003.